Designed By God

Dr. Ramona Bethany

It's is not legal to reproduce, duplicate, or transmit any part of this document in either electronic means or printed format. Recording of this publication is strictly prohibited.

Disclaimer – This book is not intended to diagnose or treat depression, anxiety, trauma or any mental or physical illness. If you are experiencing problems that interfere with your daily life reach out to your doctor or mental health professional.

Copyright © 2025 Dr. Ramona Bethany

All rights reserved

ACKNOWLEDGEMENTS

To Pastor Jason McClendon and my church family at Community Church of God of Macon Georgia, thank you for your support and the opportunity to serve God with you. Special thanks to First Lady Sylvia McClendon for encouraging me to write this book.

To Bishop Robert Culp and my church family at First Church of God Toledo Ohio, thank you for helping to shape me according to God's design into the minister I am today. To my brother Michael and my sister-in-love Lena, thank you for making the publishing of this book possible and thank you Lena for designing such a marvelous cover. Michael, your example and encouragement is greatly appreciated.

To all my relatives and friends, thank you for your love and support. Most of all to my Lord and Savior Jesus Christ, thank you for giving me the words to write and for life abundant.

TABLE OF CONTENTS

1 Designed Uniquely (Psalm 139:14)

2 Designed on Purpose (Ephesians 2:10)

3 Designed to Prosper (3 John 2)

4 Designed to Be Thankful (Col*. 3:15b)

5 Designed to Be Saved (1 Timothy 2:3-4)

6 Designed to Connect (Psalm 68:6)

7 Designed to Serve (Mark 10:45)

8 Designed to Submit (James 4:7)

9 Designed to Have Faith (Acts 27:25)

10 Designed to Grow (2 Pet 3:18)

11 Designed to Pray (Luke 18:1)

12 Designed to Choose Life (Deu*. 30:19)

13 Designed to Rejoice (Philippians 4:4)

14 Designed to Live Abundantly (John 10:10)

15 Designed to Enjoy (1 Timothy 6:17)

16 Designed to Laugh (Proverbs 17:22)

17 Designed to Win (1 Corinthians 9:24)

18 Designed to Overcome (Romans 8:37)

19 Designed to Forgive (Colossians 3:13)

20 Designed to Fellowship (1 John 1:7)

21 Designed to Fight (2 Corinthians 10:4)

22 Designed to Persevere (Gal 6:9)

23 Designed to Trust God (Pr 3:5-6)

24 Designed to Be Filled (Galatians 5:20)

25 Designed to Have Peace (John 14:27)

26 Designed to Praise God (1 Peter 2:9)

27 Designed to Speak Life (Pr 18:21)

28 Designed to Rest (Mark 6:31)

29 Designed to Worship (John 4:23)

30 Designed to Worship Corporate (Psa 34:)

31 Designed to Love (1 John 4:11)

Preface

God's Design for You 31 Day Devotional was specifically written for the Georgia Fellowship Women's Ministry Spring Conference 2025. I had the distinct pleasure of being one of the speakers for the 2024 Conference—Refreshed By the Water, held in Savannah GA. In preparation for that conference the Lord gave me some material that was placed in a pamphlet and included with the conference handouts. It was well-received and I was encouraged by Sylvia McClendon, the current President of the Georgia Fellowship Women's Ministry to write a book on this year's conference theme—Designed By God.

It has been an honor to receive a Word from the Lord to encourage and equip the wonderful women who attend this conference. Although written with the conference in mind, the scriptures apply to anyone who desires to know God as revealed through His Word. May God's design be shown in our lives as we continue to live for Him, fulfilling the purpose of His Design.

Introduction

You are a masterpiece, designed on purpose for God's purpose. The intent of this devotional is to highlight God's design for our lives. God was intentional when He created us that's why I like the New Living Translation of Ephesians 2:10 particularly the first clause of the verse—" *For we are God's masterpiece.'.* A lot of care, effort, intention and attention goes into creating a masterpiece. As described in the verses of scripture used in this devotional, a lot of care, effort, intention and attention has gone into creating us as well. What a blessing to know that we are not a mistake, an accident or a fluke of nature. God had a specific purpose in mind when He created each of us. Unfortunately, many of us do not know God's purpose nor His design for our lives. Hopefully reading this devotional will help those who struggle with knowing who they are as well as those who are seeking guidance on what God desires for us to do with our lives.

The verses highlighted in this devotional focus on God's design, His plan for our lives. The Bible is full of verses that describe the amazing way God has created us and the reason He created us. A few of those verses make up this book. May you be inspired to search for other verses as well.

I have found using a daily devotional to be helpful in a number of ways, it blesses me by keeping me focused on God's Word (like the person in Psalm 1). Using a daily devotional particularly in the morning, sets the tone for the rest of the day especially when I can connect what I read with something that occurs later in the day. But this devotional can be read at any time during the day even at night. The goal is to have a consistent holy habit of reading God's Word. Since this devotional is written around a specific topic, I would suggest reading it along with your usual devotional if you already have one that you are using. After all, we can never get too much of God's Word and it only takes less than five minutes to read the daily entry. Another benefit of using a daily devotional is it helps us to "grow in grace and the knowledge of our Lord and Savior Jesus Christ (2 Peter 3:18)" But most importantly, using a daily devotional helps us stay connected to God and I've found that time spent with God is time well spent A devotional provides an excellent means of engaging in two-way conversation with God. He speaks to us through the selected verse of scripture and we respond to Him in prayer. The format of this devotional includes a daily verse, commentary and a closing prayer. The approach that I have found helpful is Read—Reflect—Respond. Read the assigned verse and commentary, reflect on what has been read, and respond with prayer and action. If I had more space, I would have included Points to Ponder as well as Next Steps suggestions. But since I didn't have the space, I encourage you to think about what has been written and pray about how to respond with action.

May the sentence prayer at the end of each entry serve as a prayer prompt inspiring your own prayerful response. That is the goal—to be doers of God's Word and not just hearers or readers.

I have included space at the end of this devotional for the reader to prayerfully design a Plan of Action for applying what has been read. This is especially important when we read about God's design and his purpose for our lives. That's what it says in Ephesians 2:10 that He has created to do "good things He planned for us". As we understand how He designed us may we also be motivated to carry out His plan and His purpose.

How to Get the Most from This Devotional:

1. **Read the assigned verse**. For further study, read the entire chapter where the verse is taken from.

2. **Reflect, think about** the comments following the verse. What stands out to you? What catches your attention? How does it apply to your life? What changes need to be made to further reveal God's design for you and in you?

3. **Respond**. First with prayer—asking God to speak to you through the verse and devotional thought. Ask God how to put into action what has been read. Thank Him for His design for your life.

I PRAISE YOU
BECAUSE I AM
FEARFULLY AND
WONDERFULLY MADE;
YOUR WORKS ARE
WONDERFUL, I KNOW
THAT FULL WELL.

Psalm 139:10 NIV

DAY ONE

You Are A Designer's Original

I will praise You because I have been remarkably and wonderfully made. Your works are wonderful, and I know this very well
Psalms 139:14 HCS

There are approximately 200 billion trillion stars in the universe and each one is unique! Just as amazing, there are 8.2 billion unique individuals on earth and you are one of them! Our marvelous creator specializes in one of a kind creation. In our society, people spend billions of dollars on designer originals or limited editions such as purses, shoes or fragrances. But none of these products are as valuable as God's creation—you and I.

In Psalm 139, David recognized his uniqueness and praised God for his creation. Let us follow David's example and praise God for the beauty of who we are. Let us stop comparing ourselves to others or finding fault with our flaws. Instead let's allow God to shine through us just the way we are, recognizing that our imperfections accent our uniqueness. Our unique combination of physical attributes, abilities, and experiences makes us special and priceless. God created each of us on purpose and for a purpose—to glorify Him by being whom He created us to be.

Thank you, Lord, for the beauty you created in us, help us to shine brightly for you.

DAY TWO

Designed on Purpose For Purpose

For we are God's masterpiece. He has created us anew in Christ Jesus, so we can do the good things he planned for us long ago. **Ephesians 2:10 NLT**

A "masterpiece", a "designer's original", a one-of-a-kind creation! Wow!!! What a blessing to be uniquely created to carry out God's plan and purpose for our lives. When I think of a masterpiece, I think of an object of beauty, something special, and that is what we are. But we have not been created to be placed on a wall and admired like a piece of art. No, we have been designed to "do good things". We have a function to carry out, a task to complete and we discover what that specific function is when we spend time with God and follow His Word.

Three of those "good things" that God has designed for us to do are—to read His Word (Psalm 1), pray for ourselves and others (1 Timothy 2:1), and to love God, ourselves and others (Matthew 22:37-39). When we do these three things, we experience beauty in another way. This is God's design and its very good.

Father, thank you for how you created us, may your purpose be fulfilled in our lives.

DAY THREE

Designed to Prosper

Beloved, I pray that you may prosper in all things and be in health, just as your soul prospers. **3 John 1:2**

Prosperity is defined as a condition of being successful and thriving. It is often thought of as being financially successful. But God's design for us is to "prosper in all things". That is to thrive financially, physically, mentally, emotionally, relationally and spiritually. To succeed in every area of our lives. This kind of success is only possible when we put God first (Matthew 6:33). We thrive not by pursuing things, but by pursuing God and His Will for our lives.

I believe its ok to have nice things but it's important to not allow things to have us—in other words to become so consumed with "stuff" (money, prestige, fancy cars, houses and land) that we neglect our relationship with God. His Word tells us that if we delight ourselves in Him, He will give us the desires of our heart (Psalm 37:4). May the desires of our heart be to draw closer to God and to keep Him first in our actions and affections, then we will be prosperous in all things.

Father, teach "us" how to keep you first, and to not focus on getting "stuff" to the neglect of our relationship with you!

DAY FOUR
Designed to Be Thankful

And always be thankful. Colossians 3:15b

Developing and maintaining an attitude of gratitude requires intention and attention. It is so easy to start grumbling and complaining when faced with problems, setbacks and disappointments. However, the above verse reminds us that God desires us to always be thankful. How is this possible? I believe it starts with recognizing that we always have something to be thankful for.

Even in the midst of hurts and pains, illnesses, financial struggles, relationship problems, and all of life's many challenges, there is still something to be thankful for. We may not feel thankful, but we can still be thankful because gratitude is more than a feeling. I believe thankfulness is a disposition—a way of being and a discipline.

We learn to cultivate gratitude, learning like Joseph to see the "good' that God is bringing out of the bad (Gen 50:20). And so, in everything, we give thanks for it is God's will for our lives. We can always thank God for His perfect will because He knows best. We can also thank Him for His love because nothing can separate us from His love (Romans 8:38). We can especially thank Him for His presence because He promised never to leave us nor forsake us (Hebrews 13:5). And with His presence is His power and provision. **Thank you, Lord!**

DAY FIVE

Designed to Be Saved

__3__ For this is good and acceptable in the sight of God our Savior, __4__ who desires all men to be saved and to come to the knowledge of the truth. 1 Timothy 2:3-4

The beginning of chapter two of First Timothy, Paul instructs Timothy to pray for all men (v1) and for those in authority (v2). And then he explains that God "desires all men to be saved" This is God's plan for our lives—that we would be saved from sin and having a living, vibrant relationship with Him. Sin separates us from God. That is why God sent Jesus to die for our sins—to pay the penalty for our sins, so that our sins could be forgiven. Romans 6:23 tells us that

"For the wages of sin is death, but the gift of God is eternal life in Christ Jesus our Lord." Understanding God's plan and purpose for our lives begins with acknowledging our sins and obtaining forgiveness through believing Jesus Christ.

if you haven't asked God to forgive your sins and to come into your heart—do it today. This makes it possible to experience the rest of God's design for your life. To experience His forgiveness, His power, His blessings, His love, His presence and so much more. If you have accepted Christ as your Savior, then follow Paul's instruction and pray for those who don't know Christ that they might experience God's will also.

Father, thank you for sending Jesus and saving our souls.

DAY SIX

Designed to Connect

And the eye cannot say to the hand, "I have no need of you"; nor again the head to the feet, "I have no need of you." 1 Corinthians 12:21 NKJ

Since the beginning of time, God's plan was for us to live life connected to others and not alone. But also, since the beginning of time, people have struggled in their relationships with others. Remember Cain and Abel, Sarah and Hagar, Esau and Jacob, just to name a few? Fast forward to today and we all know that relationship problems continue, even among our church family and especially among the sisters!

But despite the challenges, God desires us to stay connected to others. And when we work past our differences and allow Him to heal our so-called "church hurt", we find that some of our greatest blessings can be found in our relationships with our church sisters.

So, let's resist the desire to go our separate ways when our feelings are hurt or there's a disagreement. When possible let's work past our differences and remember that God blesses unity and coming and staying together. Let's not live life in silos, on our own, separated from others. Let's stay connected.

Father, help us enjoy the blessings that come from being in your family. May we stay connected so we might be a blessing to others also.

DAY SEVEN
Designed to Serve

For even the Son of Man did not come to be served, but to serve, and to give his life as a ransom for many."

Mark 10:45 NIV

"How can I help you?" is a question we are frequently asked when we go to a store, restaurant, or some other business. But it's not a question we hear very often in church. As followers of Christ we have been called and equipped to serve others. God has blessed us with gifts, talents, abilities and resources. He has blessed us to be a blessing.

Opportunities to serve are abundant, both inside and outside the local church. As well as within and outside of our families. Whether it's ushering, singing, visiting the sick, or feeding the hungry. Sometimes it may seem overwhelming, trying to serve our families and others as well. But whenever and wherever we can be a blessing by serving others we follow Jesus example and bring glory to God.

When we seek not to be served but to serve others, God has a special way of sending others to help serve us. Let us be God's hands and feet and touch the lives of others with His love. That's our motivation and our reward.

Lord, help me to be like Jesus and seek not to be served, but to serve others for your glory.

DAY EIGHT

Designed to Submit

Therefore, submit to God. Resist the devil and he will flee from you. James **4:7**

Submission can be challenging, especially in our relationships. When it comes to our personal relationships, submission to authority is challenging because we don't like the idea of someone else telling us what to do. Sometimes it's difficult to submit because we don't trust others to treat us fairly or when we did submit we were mistreated. Unfortunately, these bad experiences influence how we submit to God. We have difficulty trusting Him, we are unsure of what will happen or we are afraid of others seeing us as weak and taking advantage of our submission.

But the previous verse in James chapter 4 tells us that God gives us grace generously (v6). And it is because of His grace that we are able to submit to God and to others. God's grace is sufficient for every situation we may encounter (2 Corinthians 12 :9).

His grace is unmerited favor and divine enablement. It empowers us to do what we cannot do in our own strength. So, we can submit to others, knowing that God is trustworthy and will protect us and bless us. We follow Jesus example and pray, "not my will, but your will be done". God's will is best and He can be trusted.

Father, may your will be done on earth in our lives.

DAY NINE

Designed to Have Faith

So, keep up your courage, men, for I have faith in God that it will happen just as he told me. Acts 27:25

"Have faith in God" is what Jesus has instructed us to do (Mark 11:22). Faith is essential for our salvation and to live this Christian life (Ephesians 2:8; Romans 1:17). Faith is especially critical during times of testing and suffering. Acts 27 records Paul's stormy journey to Rome. While traveling to Rome as a prisoner, the ship Paul was on was caught up in a severe storm for several days. When others panicked, Paul received a word from the Lord that he shared with them providing peace and reassurance. After two weeks they were shipwrecked but everyone survived and made it to land.

What stands out to me from this experience is when Paul says "I have faith in God that it will happen just as he told me." I want to respond this way when I face life's storms. To have faith that God will fulfill His Word, that He will keep His promises to me. Life can be hard with many different kinds of storms (illness, financial, spiritual, emotion) that may last for a long period of time. But God is faithful and will bring us out safely.

Father, help us to trust you during life's storms.

DAY TEN
Designed to Grow

but grow in the grace and knowledge of our Lord and Savior Jesus Christ. 2 Peter 3:18

All living things are designed to grow. But growth doesn't happen automatically, it requires participation on our part. To grow physically, we must eat nutritious meals. To grow spiritually, we must eat God's Word. Snacking instead of eating healthy food regularly or not eating consistently will result in poor health and even death. The same is true spiritually, eating a spiritual snack on Sundays may keep us alive but it won't promote healthy spiritual growth.

If we want to grow into mature Christians, we must consume God's Word daily. There are six ways that we consume God's Word that ensure healthy spiritual growth. We must hear God's Word, read it, meditate on it, memorize it, study it and apply it. When we make these actions part of our daily lives, we will grow and get to know Christ more intimately. The more we eat of God's Word, the more Christ is revealed to us and through us. Let's not skip any spiritual meals. Let's feast on God's Word and grow into mature believers.

Father, help us to eat fully and consistently on your Word and to grow more life Christ every day.

DAY ELEVEN
Designed to Pray

One day Jesus told his disciples a story to show that they should always pray and never give up. Luke 18:1

"Always pray and never give up". Words of instruction and encouragement. In Luke 18, Jesus tells the parable of the persistent widow, who kept appealing to a judge for justice. The details regarding the widow's situation are not given because the main point is what Jesus states in the beginning of the story that we should "Always pray and never give up" These instructions remind me of Paul's instructions in Philippians 4:6-7 NLT "*6 Don't worry about anything; instead, pray about everything. Tell God what you need, and thank him for all he has done. 7 Then you will experience God's peace, which exceeds anything we can understand.*

His peace will guard your hearts and minds as you live in Christ Jesus.

I'm also reminded of the lyrics from the hymn What A Friend We Have in Jesus—" *oh what peace we often forfeit, oh what needless pain we bear all because we do not carry everything to God in prayer*"

And so, we pray always and about everything. We keep praying, trusting God to answer our prayers according to His will (1 John 5:14). We don't give up because He has promised that we will be rewarded if we don't give up (Galatians 6:9).

Father, help us to be persistent in prayer, trusting that you always come through for us.

DAY TWELVE
Designed to Choose Life

This day I call the heavens and the earth as witnesses against you that I have set before you life and death, blessings and curses. Now choose life, so that you and your children may live. Deuteronomy 30:19

Making the right choice is so important. The setting for today's verse is the Israelites are preparing to cross over into the Promised Land and among the instructions that Moses gives them, we find this verse. God was encouraging His people to make the right choice. Just like the Israelites, we are faced with many choices and the decisions we make will not only impact us but future generations as well.

Choosing life is always the right choice and fullness of life is only found in Jesus Christ. (John 10:10). When we choose to give our life to Him, we are choosing to follow Him daily, thereby choosing life again and again. We never stop having to make the right choice. Whether it's in how we treat others or choosing to be honest or choosing to go forward in faith, choosing to do the right thing even when it's hard. God provides the grace and the strength to make the right choice. Blessings result when we choose to obey and follow God's Word. Today and every day, may we choose life and follow Jesus.

Father, thank you helping us make the right choice.

DAY THIRTEEN
Designed to Rejoice

Rejoice in the Lord always. Again I will say rejoice!
Philippians 4:4

Rejoice means to return to Joy or to return to the source of our Joy. Jesus repeatedly expressed that He wanted His followers to have joy— *"These things I have spoken to you, that My joy may remain in you, and that your joy may be full.* (John 15:11), *Until now you have asked nothing in My name. Ask, and you will receive, that your joy may be full. (*John 16:24). *But now I come to You, and these things I speak in the world, that they may have My joy fulfilled in themselves.* (John 17:13).

This is God's design for us, but life has a way of stealing our Joy. Whether its financial challenges, illness, relationship problems, when we focus on our problems our experience of joy begins to fade. That's why it's important to rejoice always—to get back to the source of our joy, Jesus Christ.

Praising God is the best way to rejoice and we can praise Him, no matter what we are going through. The verse that helps me to do this is Psalm 34:1 *I will bless the LORD at all times; His praise shall continually be in my mouth.* I intentionally make the choice to rejoice, to praise God and as I praise God, I gain victory over my problems and get back to Joy.

Father, thank you for a joy that can't be taken away.

DAY FOURTEEN
Designed to Live Abundantly

The thief does not come except to steal, and to kill, and to destroy. I have come that they may have life, and that they may have it more abundantly. John 10:10

Andrae Crouch's song "You Ain't Livin" says "you may be a ruler or a king, you may have the best of everything. You may be a millionaire cause the Father made it so. But here's one thing He wants the world to know, you anit' living until you've met the Savior, had a personal experience with the Savior. Until you answer His call, you ain't livin at all." These lyrics emphasize the truth that real life is only found in Jesus Christ. Unless a person has a relationship with Jesus Christ, they are merely existing and not living.

Jesus promises life abundant, life in its fullness. But the enemy of our souls, works overtime to make us settle for less than God's best.

When we allow him, Satan steals our joy, kills our witness, and destroys God's design for our lives. Fortunately, Jesus destroys the works of the Devil (1 John 3:8) and not only gives us power to defeat Satan, but also enables us to live life full and overflowing. What a blessing! Let's not allow the enemy to cheat us out of God's design or rob us of Gods' many blessings. Let's live our best life now!

Father, thank you for abundant, eternal, everlasting life, here, now, and in the future.

DAY FIFTEEN
Designed to Enjoy

Command those who are rich in this present age not to be haughty, nor to trust in uncertain riches but in the living God, who gives us richly all things to enjoy. **1 Timothy 6:17**

We live in a very materialistic society that promotes the idea that riches equals happiness. When you're rich you can afford to enjoy "stuff" like cars, houses, clothes, watches, jewelry, and money itself. But the enjoyment that these things bring does not last, that's why we are always wanting more and always pursuing the newest, the biggest, and the brightest material things cannot produce lasting satisfaction because we were designed to experience something greater. But even to be able to have material things is a blessing from God.

Hallmark has a slogan that says, "when you care enough to send the very best." This slogan reminds me of our Heavenly Father who gives good gifts (Matthew 7:11) and has sent the very best gift—Jesus Christ (John 3:16).

Although we might find momentarily pleasure in this world's riches, lasting joy is only possible through Christ. I like how David said it in Psalm 16:11, "in Your (God's) presence is fullness of joy, at Your (God's) right hand are pleasures forevermore.

Father, thank you for all that you give us, most of all thank you for Jesus Christ.

THE LORD HAS MADE EVERYTHING FOR HIS OWN PURPOSE...

Proverbs 16:4 GWT

DAY SIXTEEN
Designed to Laugh

A cheerful heart is good medicine, but a crushed spirit dries up the bones. Proverbs 17:22 NIV

In his book, "The God Prescription," neurosurgeon, Dr. Avery Jackson describes how laughter improves our health and prevents disease. Research has shown that laughter lowers blood pressure, releases muscle tension, increases feel-good hormones such as dopamine and endorphins, decreases stress hormones, boosts the immune system, burns calories and provides an over-all sense of well-being. Many of us may not be aware of the power of laughter. It is a God given ability that adds flavor to our lives.

Dr. Jackson gives the following recommendations for increasing laughter in our lives: Laugh, even when you don't feel like it. Watch or listen to funny shows or Christian comedians, read the comics, and watch funny videos.

I'll add an additional recommendation—be intentional and find something to laugh about every day. Even though life has its serious moments and even painful experiences, there is still a time to weep and a time to laugh (Ecclesiastes 3:4); So, let's laugh.

Father, thank you for the ability to laugh

DAY SEVENTEEN
Designed to Win

You know that many runners enter a race, and only one of them wins the prize. So, run to win! I Corinthians 9:24

Perhaps you've seen someone place their fingers in the shape of an "L" on their forehead, representing the word—Loser. This label does not apply to us as followers of Christ, because in Christ, we always win! We still have to run the race of life, but we run with endurance, keeping our eyes on Jesus, the author and finisher of our faith (Heb 12:2). There may be times when we feel like giving up or we may stumble and fall, but let's get back up again and win the race.

Jesus shows us how to win and what it means to be a winner. Following His example, and empowered by His Spirit, we persevere past pain and problems, overcome obstacles, and keep our eyes on the prize. We "press on to reach the end of the race and receive heavenly prize for which God, through Christ

Jesus, is calling us" (Phil 3:14 NLT).

Instead of focusing on how difficult the race may be or how weary we may feel, let's keep our minds on Him, knowing He provides the strength we need and the promise of victory that keeps us going (Heb 12:3).

Father, thank you for making us winners, help us to press on and receive our prize.

AND WE KNOW THAT ALL THINGS WORK TOGETHER FOR GOOD TO THOSE WHO LOVE GOD, TO THOSE WHO ARE THE CALLED ACCORDING TO *HIS* PURPOSE.

Romans 8:28

DAY EIGHTTEEN
Designed to Overcome

No, in all these things we are more than conquerors through him who loved us.

Romans 8:37

It doesn't take long to realize that in this life there will be troubles and trials, pain and problems. Jesus told us to expect tribulation (John 16:33). But he also told us to be of "good cheer". We may not be able to avoid hurtful situations, but we are able to be victorious and not victims.

Victorious living begins with maintaining a positive perspective. Choosing to see life as "half full instead of half empty". It doesn't deny our problems or pretend that there is no pain. But intentionally chooses to focus on the good instead of the bad, and remembers such long-held tenets and promises as "trouble don't last always" and "weeping may endure for a night but joy comes in the morning" (Psalm 30:5).

These are more than nice sayings but are reminders that help us to overcome obstacles and face life's problems. God not only provides promises to help us but He also provides power (strength) when we need it most. The Holy Spirit provides the mental, spiritual and even physical ability to overcome whatever comes our way.

With God we are more than conquerors, we are overcomers.

Father, thank you for power to overcome.

FOR IT IS GOD WHO WORKS IN YOU TO WILL AND TO ACT IN ORDER TO FULFILL HIS GOOD PURPOSE.

(Phil 2:10)

DAY NINETEEN

Designed to Forgive

Bear with each other and forgive one another if any of you has a grievance against someone. Forgive as the Lord forgave you.
Colossians 3:13

Forgiven, such a precious word when we experience forgiveness for our sins and are restored to right relationship with God. But when we are required to be the giver of forgiveness instead of the recipient, it becomes more challenging. I guess that's why Peter asked Jesus how many times we are required to forgive others (Matthew 18:21-22). No matter the offense, no matter even if the offender desires not to be forgiven. As followers of Christ, we are required to forgive as we have been forgiven.

The Amplified translation of the first part of this verse says "bearing graciously with one another". This forms the basis of our forgiveness-Grace. Grace has been described as receiving what we don't deserve—unmerited favor. We didn't deserve God's forgiveness and sometimes we didn't even desire it. But He has provided forgiveness despite our mindset or attitude. We need to follow His example. So even when it's hard, with God's power we forgive. We give what we have received, remembering the cost Jesus paid for our forgiveness.

Father, thank you for forgiveness, help us to forgive others.

DAY TWENTY
Designed to Fellowship

But if we walk in the light as He is in the light, we have fellowship with one another, and the blood of Jesus Christ His Son cleanses us from all sin. 1 John 1:7

As followers of Christ, we move from walking in darkness into walking in the Light of God's love. While walking in the light, we receive cleansing but we also receive fellowship with others who are walking in God's light as well. It's such a blessing to experience life with other believers. We are all on this journey together. Sometimes we may bump into each other or get in each other's way. But it's still a blessing to not to have to travel alone. God has graciously provided fellow travelers so we can encourage, support and edify each other. We have so much to share.

That's the benefit of fellowship, we get to share our resources—time, talents and treasures with others and they do the same with us. We also get to share our testimony—what God has done and is doing in our lives and hear the testimony of others. Let's resist any tendency to go off by ourselves but let's continue to walk with God and with others and enjoy the journey.

Father, thank you for delivering us from darkness, cleansing us and providing companions on life's journey.

DAY TWENTY-ONE
Designed to Fight

There's a war going on, not just in some
The weapons we fight with are not the weapons of the world. On the contrary, they have divine power to demolish strongholds. Corinthians 10:4 foreign land, but in the spiritual realm *(Ephesians 6:18).*

The enemy of our souls wants to defeat us, to prevent us from experiencing all God has for us. He comes to steal, kill and destroy (John 10:10) and is very strategic and crafty as he attacks us. Fortunately, we are not defenseless against his arracks. The greater one is inside us and God has provided armor to protect us (1 John 4:4; Ephesians 6:10-18) and powerful weapons for us to fight with. As soldiers in the army of the Lord, if we are going to be victorious we must not be afraid to fight.

Yes, our enemy is powerful, but with the weapons God has provided we are able to demolish strongholds of fear, and doubt as we fight the good fight of faith. Let's become skillful at using the weapons of prayer, praise, God's Word, and the name of Jesus. With these weapons, our victory is guaranteed.

Father, train our hands for war and our fingers for battle, clothe us with your armor and help us not cower under the enemy's attack but help us to demolish strongholds and praise you for the victory.

DAY TWENTY-TWO

Designed to Persevere

So, let's not get tired of doing what is good. At just the right time we will reap a harvest of blessing if we don't give up. Galatians 6:9

Often, I find myself quoting the phrase, "It's a pressing way"! I've come to realize in this life, things don't happen when or how I desire for things to happen and often I have to press pass fear, weakness, weariness, obstacles, people and problems to reach God's blessings. Just like the farmer who has to sow the seed, nourish and care for the crops before harvesting, there is a process to reaping some of God's blessings. Some blessings don't seem to require much effort on our part—we wake up every morning, most of us are able to think and walk and talk, these are all blessings bestowed on us by our loving Father.

But other blessings require effort on our part. To receive some spiritual, financial and even physical breakthroughs, we have to continue to do the right things-pray, believe, and obey.

But the harvest of blessing is coming when we persevere and cooperate with God. It's important for us to not give up or give in but also as verse 10 instructs us, as we have opportunity, to do good to all people, especially to those pressing toward the blessing.

Father, help us press on to the harvest of blessing.

DAY TWENTY-THREE
Designed to Trust God

__5__ Trust in the Lord with all your heart, And lean not on your own understanding; __6__ In all your ways acknowledge Him, And He shall direct your paths. Proverbs 3:5-6

"In God We Trust" is printed on US currency and even on some license plates. More than seeing it several times a day, we have opportunity to put it into practice. Whether its trusting God for healing, finances, strength, peace, blessings, or spiritual breakthrough, living life requires that we trust God. But for some of us, trust doesn't come easy. Probably because we've had experiences where we put our trust in others and they failed us. But God never fails.

Another hinderance to trusting God, is when we're trying to figure how things are going to work out. Today's verse reminds us to "lean not on our own understanding."

Life has many challenges that we won't be able to figure out. Instead we need to "acknowledge him in all our ways". The Message Version of this verse says, "Listen for God's voice in everything you do, everywhere you go; he's the one who will keep you on track". God's Voice found in His Word shows us how to trust Him—one day at a time, one situation at a time, one need at a time. He can be depended on because He always comes through.

Father, thank you that we can always trust you.

DAY TWENTY-FOUR

Designed to Be Filled

Don't be drunk with wine, because that will ruin your life. Instead, be filled with the Holy Spirit,
Galatians 5:20 NLT

The book of Acts is filled with examples of New Testament believers being filled with the Holy Spirit (Acts 2:4; 4:8,31; 11:24;13:9; 13:52) To be filled with the Holy Spirit is to be empowered and controlled by the Holy Spirit. This is what Jesus promised His followers that they would receive the Holy Spirit's power (Acts 1:8). This is essential if we are going to live a Godly life. It is only through the Holy Spirit's power that we are able to produce the fruit of love, joy, peace, patience, goodness, kindness, faithfulness, gentleness and self - control.

Being filled with the Holy Spirit requires that we surrender our total selves—mind, body, and emotions to Him. As the disciples were filled with the Holy Spirit they were able to accomplish great exploits for God. The same is true for us, when we are empowered by the Holy Spirit, He produces the character of Christ within us and equips to serve God in amazing ways.

Father, fill us with Your Spirit so we can become like you and do great things for your glory.

DAY TWENTY-FIVE
Designed to Have Peace

Peace I leave with you, My peace I give to you; not as the world gives do I give to you. Let not your heart be troubled, neither let it be afraid.

John 14:27

In the midst of life's chaos and confusion, Jesus provides us with peace in at least two ways. First because of Christ, we have peace with God. We were once separated from God because of sin. Now our relationship has been restored because of Christ's dying for our sins. Romans 5:1 tells us—" Therefore, having been justified by faith, we have peace with God through our Lord Jesus Christ," Secondly, we have access to the Peace of God through prayer.

Philippians 4:6-7 instructs us "Be anxious for nothing, but in everything by prayer and supplication, with thanksgiving, let your requests be made known to God; **7** and the peace of God, which surpasses all understanding, will guard your hearts and minds through Christ Jesus. The "peace of God which surpasses all understanding" is perfect peace which the Lord provides as we keep our minds on Him (Isaiah 26:3). Let's not allow fear and trouble to rob us of the peace that only Christ can provide.

Father, thank you for your peace which the world cannot take away.

DAY TWENTY-SIX

Designed to Praise God

But you are a chosen generation, a royal priesthood, a holy nation, His own special people, that you may proclaim the praises of Him who called you out of darkness into His marvelous light; 1 Peter 2:9

Scriptures tell us that we were created to praise God (Isaiah 43:21), and He is worthy of all praise. We praise Him for His goodness, His faithfulness, mercy, provision, grace and love, just to name a few things. Individually we can praise Him for salvation, for protection, mercy, healing and so much more. We not only praise Him for all the wonderful things He has done but when we think of how awesome He is, it results in praise.

What an honor and privilege to offer praise to God. And as the saying goes, "when praises go up, blessings come down." It's just like when we give to God He gives back to us. Which makes us want to praise Him even more. The Hymn says it best, "I will praise Him, Hallelujah, I will praise Him more and more if I had ten thousand lives in which to praise Him, I could not my precious Lord adore.

Thank you, Lord, for all you have done for us. Help us to make your praise glorious.

DAY TWENTY-SEVEN
Designed to Speak Life

Death and life are in the power of the tongue,
And those who love it will eat its fruit.
Proverbs 18:21

The power of our words should never be underestimated. Our words can hurt or help and heal. Our words can speak life or death. Because our words are so powerful we should be slow to speak and quick to listen (James 1:19), The acronym T.H.I.N.K. before you speak, provides good guidelines for monitoring what we say. It is suggested that before we speak we ask ourselves, is what I'm going to say—T (true), H(Helpful), I (Inspiring), N (Necessary), or K (Kind.)? Very few people stop to think about what they say to others until after they've said something that they wish they hadn't.

Even if we don't evaluate what we say, it would be helpful just to follow the guideline of speaking life—speaking words of encouragement every time we have the opportunity. What a difference it would make if everyone would choose to speak words filled with grace. (Ephesians 4:6. Let's make it our goal every day.

Father may my words and thoughts be pleasing to you and pleasant to those who hear them.

DAY TWENTY-EIGHT
Designed to Rest

Then Jesus said, "Let's go off by ourselves to a quiet place and rest awhile." Mark 6:31 NLT

Most of us are familiar with the abbreviation "RIP" which is often see on gravestones and stands for "rest in peace." Although we think of "rest in peace" as applying to those who have passed, it can also apply to those who are alive as well.

As followers of Christ, we can have rest and lasting peace even in the midst of the chaos of our busy everyday lives. Resting in Jesus, involves learning how to be content (Philippians 4:11). It also involves not stressing ourselves out over getting things done or pursuing getting things—keeping up with the latest trends and demands on our time. Instead we learn to slow down, to "come aside* before we come apart". We build into our schedule's times of rest, relaxation, refreshing and renewal.

Daily moments of refreshing in addition to our normal times of sleep—are an essential part of self-care. Even in our busiest times like what Jesus and his disciples were experiencing in this occasion recorded in Mark 6, let's get quiet, take some deep breaths and rest mentally, spiritually and physically.

Father, may we learn to rest in You.

* come aside—Mark 6:31 KJV

DAY TWENTY-NINE
Designed to Worship

But the time is coming—indeed it's here now—when true worshipers will worship the Father in spirit and in truth. The Father is looking for those who will worship him that way.

John 4:23 NLT

Our God is worthy of praise, honor, and worship. The song sung years ago expresses it well—" when I think of the goodness of Jesus and all He has done for me, my soul cries our "Hallelujah, I praise God for saving me." When we think of God's goodness and greatness, we can't help but praise Him. Words seems so limited when trying to express how great God is and our appreciation for all He has done. Thankfully the Holy Spirit communicates beyond simple words (Romans 8:26) and that is why we must worship God in Spirit and in truth. Worship Him from our hearts, our minds and our mouths.

In the discussion on Worship with the Samaritan Woman recorded in John chapter 4, Jesus said the Father is looking for true worshippers (v23). God desires our worship not because He needs it but because we get lifted when we lift Him up.

May the Father find true worshippers in us, as we gather to worship with others and even when we worship Him alone in those private intimate moments. Let's recognize His greatness and give Him the praise that He is worthy of. Let's worship Him with our lips and with our lives.

Bless the LORD, O my soul. O LORD my God, You are very great; *Psalm 104:1a NIV*

DAY THIRTY

Designed to Worship Together

Oh, magnify the LORD with me, And let us exalt His name together. Psalm 34:3

Amazing things happen when God's people come together and worship. Whether it's when the singers and musicians made one sound at the dedication of the temple in Jerusalem and God's glory filled the temple (2 Chronicles 5:13-14). Or in the New Testament on the day of Pentecost when the followers of Christ were gathered together in the Upper Room and the Holy Spirit filled the place and birthed the church (Acts 2:1-4).

Whenever we come together and worship our Lord together, something powerful, something special, something amazing happens. Worship acknowledges God's presence and power within us and among us. Even in this digital age when services are streamed and people join virtually,

Magnifying God together helps us see Him as bigger than our differences and uniqueness. God joins us when we worship Him. So, I agree with the scripture's instruction for us to not forsake our assembling together (Hebrews 10:25). Let us bring our gifts and our talents and join our voices in worshipping our God because He is so worthy and we are lifted when we lift him up.

Father, you are worthy of it all, we worship you.

DAY THIRTY-ONE

Designed to Love and Be Loved

Beloved, if God so loved us, we also ought to love one another. 1 John 4:11

What a blessing, to be loved by God! Probably the most famous verse ever seen on the tv screen is John 3:16—God so loved the world, that He gave His one and only son, that whoever believes in Him should not perish but have eternal life. In a world filled with lonely people, who feel unloved, it's so important to spread the news, that God is love and He loves all of us. He has shown His love for us by sending Christ to die for our sins. Now we have an opportunity to share His love with others. Jesus said that others would know we are His disciples by our love for each other (John 13:35).

He also instructed us to love our enemies (Luke 6:35). Yes, some people are easier to love than others, *but* ultimately, we should love everybody and this is made possible because God has given us His love and will love through us (Romans 5:5). When we yield to the Holy Spirit and allow Him to produce the fruit of love in us, others will know what it means to be loved by God. Let's allow the love of God to flow everywhere we go.

Father, thank you for loving us, we give you our lives so you can love others through us.

CONCLUSION

There are so many more verses of scripture that reveal God's design in our lives and His plan and purpose for us. Perhaps we will continue to explore them in a future book. But one of the things that stood out to me, as I was writing this book, was the significance of our relationship with Jesus. So much, if not everything is connected to our relationship with Jesus Christ. We are saved and have purpose—to live for Christ (Galatians 2:20). We are thankful when we think about all the things He has done for us. We are connected to others who are connected to Him. We rejoice and live abundantly all because of Jesus. And when we think about all these blessings it leads us to worship God.

Which is why we were created. So ultimately God's plan and purpose is for Christ to live in us and through us, touching the lives of others with the love of God. It is my prayer that as we grow in our recognition and understanding of God's plan and purpose, that we will live in a such a way that builds His Kingdom and brings Him glory. The world still needs love sweet love and we can share the love of God with everyone we meet. This is the "good works" that God designed for us.

ACTION PLAN

Prayerfully respond to the following questions:

1. What part of how God has designed me stands out to me (for example, that I am designed to serve or to connect with others, or to love or to worship)?

_____
_____
_____

2. How do I see this aspect of God's design in my life? (for example, when I think about God designing me to serve Him by serving others, I volunteer at the usher, or to sing, or to pass out food, etc.). What do you do _____

_____
_____
_____
_____

3. What are three things I can do to continue to fulfill God's purpose for my life? When and with whom can I do these things?

1. _____
   _____

2.

_____
_____

3.
_____
_____

4. Write a prayer of thanksgiving and request for guidance

-
_____
_____

You Are

A Designer Original!

Created on purpose for God's Purpose!

Everything God makes is beautiful, including you!

God is glorified when we enjoy our uniqueness and carry out His plan and purpose for our lives.

Made in the USA
Monee, IL
10 February 2025